THE SIBLINGS OF KANCHIPURAM

A Garland of Poems

HARINIE JEEVITHA

Edited by Smaran Haridashwa

INDIA • SINGAPORE • MALAYSIA

To

The Consorts of
The Siblings of Kanchipuram...

CONTENTS

THE GARLAND OF POEMS

Note: Sanskrit verses have been transliterated in the IAST format. Words from other languages are italicised and have been used without diacritical marks. Names of places, people and Gods are not italicised.

INVOCATION

The very concept of the Supreme—the transcendental essence of all existence—evokes a profound sense of awe, as it elevates us beyond the mundane and monotonous. A seeker's journey towards Divinity is a playful paradox: the Infinite One, which is in itself the ultimate goal, slips into a finite garb, descends as Grace to initiate the journey, provides unwavering guidance at every step, draws the seeker closer and closer and finally, absorbs its apparent fragment into its womb of Infinity where the individual dissolves in the Indivisible.

"यमेवैष वृणुते तेन लभ्यः तस्यैष आत्मा विवृणुते तनूं स्वाम् ॥ "

"Only he, whom the Supreme chooses, can attain Him, for to him alone the Supreme Self reveals Its (formless) form", says the Kaṭhopaniṣad (1.2.23).

When the Divine chooses to manifest in the depths of one's heart, a devotee is born, and an intimate odyssey unfolds. Once the Divine has dawned within, if one focuses largely on material concerns relegating spirituality to an indefinite 'later', it is akin to waiting for the ocean's waves to subside before taking a refreshing dip. The devotee must strive to keep that heartfelt connection constantly alive through ways more than one. This can be achieved by making the Supreme the locus—the centre of every activity and emotion, thereby allowing them to be transmuted into spiritual expressions.

Devotion is a sacred alchemy that transforms even the most despicable and destructive of emotions into divine outpourings, guiding one rapidly towards the Lord. Narada Muni recounts to King Yudhishthira the diverse emotions through which devotees found their way to the Lord:

"For the Gopis of Vrindavan, it was their love; for Kamsa, it was fear; for Shishupala and the like, it was hatred; for the Yadavas, it was familial connection; for you—the Pandavas—it was affection; and for devotees like me, it was pure devotion." (Srimad Bhagavatam 7.1.30)

"tam eva śaraṇaṃ gaccha sarvabhāvena bhārata"—
"Surrender exclusively unto Him with your whole being, O Arjuna", says Lord Krishna in the Gita (18.62).

When we dedicate every aspect of our personality to the Divine and His service, our life transforms into an elaborate ritual of fervent worship and surrender.

This book is one such offering that has sprung from the womb of time, born of a devotee's desire to offer herself to the Divine through poetry, adorning the 'Siblings of Kanchipuram' with a garland of her verses.

> Poetry goes beyond mere words in place,
> It is the living breath of the Infinite's Grace.
> It is the painting that speaks in colours bright,
> It is the dance of stillness on a soulful night.

It is the freezing fire of a warrior's might,
It is the blazing river that streams upright.
It is joy's cheerful chirp of innumerable rounds,
It is the symphony of silence where peace abounds.

Poetry goes beyond mere words in place,
It is the expression of the Self in myriad ways!

A poem, with words woven around itself, is like a gift, beautifully ribbon-wrapped. The true treasure lies within: a condensation of joyous thrills, painful pangs, and serendipitous scenes concealed beneath the wrapper of words.

To uncover this treasure, you must tactfully undo the knot, unfurl the wrapper and behold the gift of poetry—a present to be savoured in the present—here and now. When you learn to transcend mere reading and truly experience poetry, you get to taste the intense feeling that the poet has breathed into every word. In that profound encounter, you lose yourself in the boundless Infinitude of the Self.

Kanchipuram is one of the most sacred centres of pilgrimage, woven with a rich spiritual and cultural heritage. All the prominent deities of the Hindu tradition have a significant presence in this town of temples. This vibrant town is a confluence of Jnana and Bhakti, of Shiva and Shakti, of Hara and Hari, of service and study—making it a spiritual haven that upholds the principle of Oneness.

Devotion and Knowledge,
Mother and Father,
Vishnu and Shiva—
Two sides of the One coin.

One refreshes, the other reforms;
One enchants, the other engrosses.
One lightens—making us fully light;
Other enlightens—making us full of light.

Different as sides, yet one as the coin,
Distinct expressions, yet in essence they join.
Diverse perspectives, yet a similar intent,
Differing in contents, yet equally content.

Devotion and Knowledge,
Mother and Father,
Vishnu and Shiva—
The One in two and the two in One!

The Siblings of Kanchipuram is a poetic outpouring of devotion that has flown through Harinie, a blessed child of the Divine Mother. The poems presented—an expression of her being in all its immensity—stand testament to her purity of intent, intensity of devotion and profundity of thought. Expressing my deepest gratitude and reverence to the Divine in her, I invoke the blessings of the Siblings of Kanchipuram and their consorts upon all of us with the following verse as we embark on this beatific expedition:

शिवं शिवां हरिं रमां सदा मुदा हृदालये
स्मरामि भावयामि नौमि लालये कृपालये ।
स्वभावनित्यशुद्धबुद्धमुक्तरूपिणां कृपा-
विशेषतो निजात्मसंस्थनित्यसत्यमाश्रये ॥

I incessantly meditate upon Shiva (Ekamreshwara Swamy), Shakti (Kamakshi Devi), Hari (Varadaraja Swamy) and Lakshmi (Perundevi Thayar) with abundant joy and devotion. I remember them, contemplate upon them, bow to them, and lovingly adore them within my heart-temple—an abode of their compassion. With the exceptional grace of these deities—manifestations of the Supreme Self, which is Eternal, Pure, Awakened and Liberated in nature—I shall take refuge and firmly abide in the Eternal Truth that resides within.

May we present our hearts, filled with reverence, as a well-decorated stage for Harinie and the Siblings of Kanchipuram to commence their enthralling dance of devotion. My prayers to Bhagavan for showering His grace in abundance upon all those connected with this book, granting them the highest good!

Arunachala Shiva!

Smaran Haridashwa
10-08-24

KANCHIPURAM

This is a popular adage which declares that the best of flowers is jasmine, the best of men is Lord Vishnu, the best of women is Rambha and the best of towns is Kanchipuram.

When I think of Kanchi, I think of its exquisite silks and *Idlis*; I think of the people who greet with a warm smile and make me feel at home, as if I were their own. When I think of Kanchi, I most certainly think of Goddess Kamakshi, Lord Varadaraja, Lord Ekamreshwara and the faded *Gopurams*, the sight of which swell the heart. I think of the spell of rains that add flavour to its already effervescent sands; I think of the rays of the sun that hit the grounds, adding glitter to its already shining lands.

Amongst the seven *Mokshapuris*—Ayodhya, Mathura, Haridwar, Kashi, Kanchi, Ujjain and Dwaraka, 'Kanchipuram' (Kanchi) is the only *Mokshapuri* situated in the southern part of India, in the state of Tamil Nadu. While Haridwar, Kashi and Ujjain are sacred to devotees of Lord Shiva; Ayodhya, Mathura and Dwaraka for devotees of Vishnu; Kanchi is considered sacred for devotees of Shakti, Vishnu and Shiva.

The origin of the name 'Kanchipuram' is predominantly attributed to two legends. Sati Devi's girdle (*Kanchi*) is said to have fallen in this place, and the other reason being that the *Ashwamedha Yagna* of Lord Brahma (*Ka*) to worship (*anchi*) Maha Vishnu was performed here, thus giving rise to the name 'Kanchipuram'. Praised as the land that fructifies penance and prayers, and owing to the lore that King Satyavrata ruled over this region, Kanchi is also commonly addressed as 'Satyavrata Kshetram'.

14 out of the 108 *Divya Desams*, 12 out of the 276 *Thevara Sthalams* and one of the most prominent *Shakti Peetas* are situated here. Saints and Acharyas such as Ramanujacharya, Thirukacchi Nambi, Thirumoolar, Appar, Sundarar, Sambandar and Adi Shankaracharya have walked this part of the earth where the Supreme Truth manifests as a triad—three divine couples—Lord Ekamreshwara & Kamakshi Devi, Lord Varadaraja & Perundevi Thayar, Lord Brahma & Saraswathi Devi (as the doer of the *Yagna* and River Vegavathi respectively), making Kanchipuram the composite coming together of Kailasa, Vaikunta and Brahmaloka.

When I think of Kanchi, I think of the flower vendors who string flowers with elan; I think of the fervour of the devotees towards their deities; I think of the warm homes with a welcoming *pyol;* and when I think of Kanchi, I think of the idyllic lives of its inhabitants steeped in simplicity.

"puṣpeṣu jātī puruṣeṣu viṣṇuḥ
nārīṣu rambhā nagareṣu kāñcī || "

SRI KAMAKSHI DEVI

Among the 51 sacred *Shakti Peetas*, Kanchipuram is a place of prime importance. When Adi Shankaracharya came to Kanchipuram at the end of his *Digvijaya*, he renovated the temples of Goddess Kamakshi, Lord Ekamreshwara and Lord Varadaraja with the help of King Rajasena. He also established the *Sri Chakra* in front of the Mother Goddess.

'Kamakshi' refers to the One with splendorous eyes, and She is the One who fulfills all our desires with Her mere glance. The noose that She holds indicates that She pulls us back on track when we go astray; the goad represents one-pointed focus; the sugarcane bow and the flower arrows symbolise the mind and the five senses, assuring protection from the control exerted by them.

Within the *Gayathri Mantapa*, on a *Peeta* that represents *Omkara*, the Goddess is seated in a cross-legged posture, wearing a crown adorned with the crescent moon. The shrine of Kamakshi Devi also has an image of the Goddess in a standing posture of meditation, with the right leg crossed over the left. To Her left resides the Goddess of wealth as 'Aroopa Lakshmi', who lost Her form and beauty on mocking Maha Vishnu. Lakshmi Devi seeks the help of the Goddess of Kanchi, who restores Her form, thereby making Kamakshi—Kamalamanohari—the enticer of Kamala's mind. To the right of Goddess Kamakshi is a small shrine for Maha Vishnu as Adi Varaha Perumal. This shrine of the Lord is known as

Thirukalvanoor and forms one of the 108 *Divya Desams.*

Kamakshi Devi is the reigning Goddess of Kanchi and the composite of all energies; therefore, there are no separate *Sannidhis* for Devi in the temples of Shiva in Kanchipuram. This manifestation of Adi Shakti bestowed the boon of speech and wisdom on Mooka Kavi, an ardent devotee of the Goddess, who penned *Mooka Panchashati,* extolling the Goddess in five cantos of hundred verses each.

"sarvakāmapradānena kāmākṣīmiti kāmataḥ ।
māṃ praṇamyātra madbhaktā labhantāṃ vāñchitaṃ varam ॥"
(Skanda Mahapuranam 1.3.4.52)

"I shall be known as Kamakshi on account of my bestowing all desires. Worshipping me here, my devotees are blessed with the fulfilment of their cherished desire."

SRI VARADARAJA PERUMAL

Divya Desams of the Srivaishnavas are 108 in number. Amongst them, Varadaraja Swamy temple, also known as Devaraja Swamy temple, situated in Kanchipuram, is one of the three foremost *Kshetrams*. After a tiff between Lord Brahma and Goddess Saraswati, as Brahma yearned to have the *Darshan* of Maha Vishnu with four arms, He performed an *Ashwamedha Yagna* in the *Homakunda* constructed by Vishwakarma in Satyavrata Kshetram—a place which yields manifold results for penance. Maha Vishnu manifested from the fire as Lord Varadaraja with a conch, discus, mace and the *Abhaya mudra* in His four arms.

Devotees flock in large numbers to have a *Darshan* of the Lord who stands atop 'Atthigiri' (an elephant hillock with 24 steps) in Kanchipuram. At the base of the hillock is a cave-like structure which forms the shrine of Lord Yoga Narasimha who is regarded as the primordial deity of the temple. For this reason, Varadaraja Swamy temple is also addressed as 'Narasimha Kshetram'.

With three outer precincts (*Prakarams*), a 100-pillared hall, 'Anantasaras' tank where the idol of 'Atthi Varadar' is stored, the temple is an architectural marvel of the Vijayanagara Empire. The consort of the Lord is Perundevi Thayar whose shrine is situated in the third *Prakaram* of the temple.

The legend of *Gajendra Moksham*, Swami Koorathazwan

being bestowed with eyesight, the *Upadesa* of the six tenets of *Vishishtadvaita* philosophy to Thirukacchi Nambi, redemption from a curse that turned two disciples of Sage Gautama into lizards, are some of the legends associated with the Lord. Azhwars, Acharyas and poets have sung the glory of the Lord in different languages, thereby spreading the essence of His benevolence in all effervescence.

Festivities are celebrated all through the year in this temple with grandeur, and the *Brahmotsavam* (annual temple festival) takes place during the Tamil month of Vaigasi. While the Lord's procession on His different mounts are a spectacle to behold, the '*Garuda Seva*', during which tens of thousands of devotees gather with ardent devotion, is an exhilarating experience where the pairs of eyes brim with tears of joy and the hearts, with the bliss of fulfilment.

Lord Varadaraja is the Emperor who bestows bountiful boons, and the devotees fervently believe that He answers all their prayers. The words '*mā śuca:*', meaning 'don't grieve', are inscribed on the right palm of the idol of the Lord who protects and bestows abundant blessings on those who surrender unto Him.

> "sarvadharmānparityajya māmekaṃ śaraṇaṃ vraja |
> ahaṃ tvā sarvapāpebhyo mokṣayiṣyāmi mā śuca: ||"
> (Bhagavad Gita 18.66)

> "Abandoning all duties, take me as your sole refuge.
> I shall liberate you from all sins; do not grieve."

FOREWORD

In the year 2022, Natyarangam, the dance wing of Narada Gana Sabha Trust, was planning to have its annual thematic Bharathanatyam event on the festivals of ten temples. Our organising committee had been impressed with young Harinie Jeevitha's solo performances and participation in the group productions of her guru Smt. Sheela Unnikrishnan. Additionally, we had observed her creativity at the Natya Sangraham, our annual camp for dancers at the temple village of Thennangur. We reached out to her to see if she would be willing to take up the challenge of creating a thematic presentation at short notice. With her guru's blessings, she took up the formidable task with enthusiasm.

Her performance, 'Varadarājam Upāsmahē' (based on the *Brahmotsavam* of Kanchipuram Varadaraja Swamy temple), at our dance festival swept everyone off their feet. There was not a dry eye when she concluded on a high point of *Sharanagati* (surrender). Single handed, she brought to life every aspect of the festival, the grandeur of the spectacle, the magic of the legends, the wave of *Bhakti* that swayed the thousands of devotees assembled, and much more. Weaving lyrics, music, *nritta* and *abhinaya* in one composite whole, she created poetry of the highest order on stage.

This book of poems is a sequel to that experience she shared with the audience on that occasion. Dance is defined as *Drishya Kavyam* (visual poetry) on account of its subtle, suggestive and evocative *abhinaya*. A dancer is required to master several allied arts such as music, knowledge of poetry and literature, of the Puranas and legends, of languages and philosophy. She or he should be able to perceive and experience poetry in their very bones to create *Rasa*. I had heard that Harinie had already published her first book of poems in English. I was deeply touched and felt honoured when she requested me to give the foreword to this book. I am convinced that Varadaraja had chosen Harinie to present His glory and had ordained our committee to facilitate the connection.

The very title of this collection *The Siblings of Kanchipuram* is indicative of Harinie's connectedness. Connected to the two deities, Kamakshi and her brother Varadaraja, and their connected grace bestowed on the *bhakta*, Harinie's spiritual leanings render the poems an experiential journey into the heart of realisation. She forges an easy relationship with the deities, where she can question them, tease them, play with them and marvel at them. The individual poems carry no titles and they can be read as a progression of one long poem on a single theme.

Kanchipuram, here, is more than just an ancient town. In poem 21, it becomes a town that is in two, Shiva Kanchi and Vishnu Kanchi.

If Shiva is verily She,
And She is verily Vishnu,
Connect the dots if you please.　　— says the poet.

Poem 18 has already pointed out the three vertical and three horizontal lines, both being just points of view, and raised the question,

Why then does the town have two halves?

In poem 20, she poses the question directly to Vishnu/ Varadaraja

Why can't You walk down further
And make our bodies Your Kanchipuram?

The body has been referred to as the *Kshetram* in the Bhagavad Gita, and here, the devotee is inviting the *Kshetrajna* to come and reside in her heart.

It is not always meditation and metaphysics. Fun and fantasy embrace the Siblings in flashes of *soulabhyam* (easy and friendly approachability).

The standing Varada takes the seated posture of Kamakshi and She, in turn, wants to stand for a while like Him. They are both tricksters and play games with the devotee. The devotee even takes pity on the one pair of eyes that is unable to witness the awe-inspiring spectacle of the *Garuda Seva* witnessed by thousands.

The story of *Gajendra Moksham* acquires new dimensions every time the lotus, the elephant and the crocodile appear in a number of poems. It reaches its climax in the refrain about the pond where, she says,

There are lotuses
There are crocodiles too.

This poem, which is one of my favourites, brings back the final moment of the scene where Harinie enacted on stage the battle between Gajendra and the crocodile. At the end, an exhausted Gajendra extends a trembling trunk with a drooping lotus as his offering to the Lord.

Many of the poems can be visualised as *abhinaya* by a consummate artist. Poem 26 describes the act of *tapas*

In that heat of the fire
He made me Dance to His Tunes.

A simple and effective diction, an easy conversational tone, a shift in perspective and a penchant for the poetic devices make the free verse form effective in its communication. The poems are an external and internal spiritual journey by a very sensitive mind that can create with equal felicity and intensity, a *Drishya Kavyam* on stage as well as on the printed page.

Sujatha Vijayaraghavan
18-7-24

PREFACE

I have had the chance to visit Kanchipuram many times along with Sheela ma'am and Shobha *akka* who took me with them during their visits to Kamakshi Amman temple. The car would arrive at my doorstep at five in the morning to pick me up. I would sleep away to glory until we reached the glorious town of white *Gopurams*—Kanchipuram.

.

.

.

In July 2021, I visited Kanchi with two of my friends. One of them suggested that we visit a few more temples too that day other than the Kamakshi temple. He took us to Varadaraja Swamy temple. But, since it was around the time when COVID-19 lockdown had just been relaxed, we were allowed only into the shrine of Perundevi Thayar. We had a *Darshan* of the Goddess and returned home.

.

.

.

In October 2021, a couple of days before the release of my first book—*Perspectives: An Illustrated Anthology*—I took a copy of the book to Kanchipuram to place it at the feet of Goddess Kamakshi. That morning, I also happened to visit Sri Maha Periyava's Mani Mantapam, where, in a surprising turn of events, the book reached the hands of Bala Periyava, who scanned through the pages for a couple of minutes, spoke a few words and walked away with the book. Thus, the book was released before it was scheduled to be released and the first copy was taken, well within Kanchipuram.

.

.

.

In the third week of March 2022, I received a phone call from Smt. Sujatha Vijayaraghavan, a writer, musicologist and art scholar. She asked me if I was interested in taking up a dance project on the *Brahmotsavam* of the Kanchipuram temple. I was thrilled when I heard "Kanchipuram". Sensing the excitement in my voice, she asked me if I had ever seen the '*Garuda Seva*' in Kanchi. For me, Kanchipuram was synonymous with Kamakshi, and Kanchipuram temple only meant Kamakshi Amman temple. So, I was puzzled, unable to connect the dots between the Goddess and Garuda! I asked her, "Ma'am, but, which temple in Kanchipuram are you referring to?" Now, it was her turn to be puzzled. She said, "Varadaraja Swamy temple, of course! Haven't you been there? Have you not heard of Atthi Varadar?"

.

.

.

On an *Ekadasi* morning in April 2022, I visited, or rather revisited Varadaraja Swamy temple in Kanchipuram. I had to weave and present a dance production on the *Brahmotsavam* of the temple and therefore had to visit the temple frequently for research purposes. During this process, it felt like the coins began to move seamlessly. People came and played their parts with passion, and I was safely reduced to a mere witness, observing the 'Happenings' from a close proximity. On August 18, 2022, 'Varadarājam Upāsmahē' was premiered at Narada Gana Sabha, Chennai. That evening was special: an evening that would stay etched in my mind even when my memory begins to ebb away.

.

.

.

Sometime around March 2023, a bunch of poems began; one by one; one after another, leaving me surprised, reducing me to a mere witness, once again. Writing poems are a matter of, if I may say so, humble instinct to me where the writing precedes my thinking. My sustained relationship with Dance and a succinct rendezvous with Literature has attracted me to Poetry. Dancing to and reading works of love, longing and lore by the Azhwars, Nayanmars, Vira-Shaivas, Varkaris and other poets have introduced me to a world where the devotee dares to engage in a one-to-one conversation with the Divine—sometimes praising, sometimes conversing, sometimes questioning, even scolding, chiding and singing songs of love.

I am only a novice in the art of poetry writing and a beginner in understanding the ancient scriptures. These poems are no proclamations, but mere perspectives—short and spontaneous—probably emerging out of fragments of experiences, emotions, questions, thoughts, facts and imagination—collected and sewn with love, over a period of time.

This anthology, that came about by sheer happenstance, is an offering presented to the 'Siblings of Kanchipuram'— Goddess Kamakshi and Lord Varadaraja. These are poems penned in free verse—some of praise, some of reprimand, some of surrender, and some of demand.

You may not agree with all that the poems say; you may not relate to some questions that I pose; you may not understand what the poems mean. But, I hope that this collection will offer you an experience—just an experience of Poetry.

The poems are ready; the poetry is yet to begin.

> For each one—their Deity,
> For each one—their Devotion,
> For each one—their Expression,
> For each one—their Experience.

“या उमा सा स्वयं विष्णुः ।”
(रुद्रहृदयोपनिषद्)

“yā umā sā svayaṃ viṣṇuḥ |”
(Rudrahṛdayopaniṣad)

She, who is Uma, is verily Vishnu.

THE SIBLINGS OF

KANCHIPURAM

1.

By focusing the mind on Her,
One attains devotion.
From devotion comes fervour;
From fervour arises determination;
Determination gives rise to discipline;
Discipline cleanses the mind.
In a mind that is clean,
There is space for wisdom to enter;
From wisdom comes realisation of the Self;
Self-realisation leads to liberation.
Focus the mind now on Her
Who is seated on the focused center point
In a cross-legged posture,
At Kanchipuram,
waiting—
To grant liberation.

2.

He is a man of grandeur,
But it is the simple things that please Him.

Offer Him melted butter,
His heart will melt for you.
Give Him a Tulsi leaf,
Watch Him come down to you.
Give Him a fistful of flattened rice,
Get sparkling palaces in return.
Offer Him a lotus—
To the One who is the Hill atop
The elephant hill in Kanchi;
Offer Him a lotus—
He will relieve you
From the Clutches of the Crocodile,
And liberate the mammoth
Elephant of Ego in you.

He is a man of grandeur,
But it is the simple things that please Him.

3.

They are tricksters.

Like a dose of the disease
That the vaccine introduces
To the body—
Warming up for the war ahead,
They do the same trickery.

Ask them for desirelessness,
They show you a taste of desire.
Plead with them for painlessness,
They introduce you to pain.
Pray to them for detachment,
And only then you will know
What it is to get attached.

They are tricksters,
The Siblings of Kanchi.
They are tricksters.

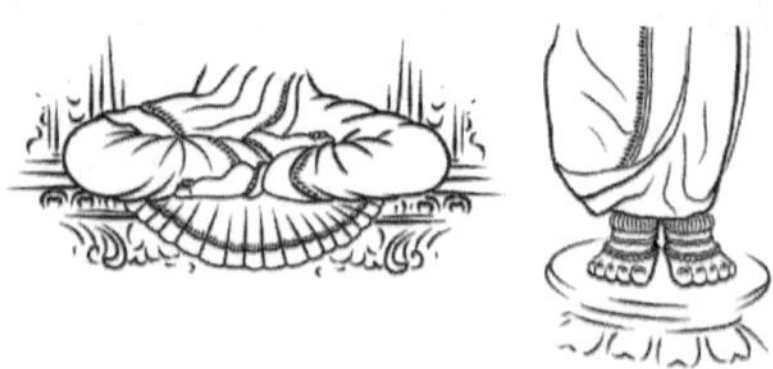

4.

Every time a poem is born
What a marvel it is:
A combination of words
That never existed before;
A force of nature coming into being,
Taking birth anew.

Whose greatness is it, then?
That of the poet?
Or of the language?
Or of words and letters?
Or of thoughts?
Inspirations?

A mute who spoke no words
Sang five times hundred verses
After being fed by Her.
She fed him with a betel leaf—
The Empress of Shiva Kanchi;
From which flowed poetry.

Every time a poem is born
What a marvel it is!

She,
From whose sidelong glance
Ideas are born;
From whose sugarcane bow
Words are born;

From whose flower arrows
Metres are born;
Is the eternal womb
Of all Poetry.

Every time a poem is born
What a marvel it is!

5.

On an *Ekadasi* morning
I met Him for the first time—
The One with a Conch,
Discus and Mace.

When the crowds were busy
Tending to the *Utsava* idol downstairs,
He was standing atop the hill—
As an idle idol: ideally waiting.

The priest ushered me
Into the sanctum.
I had only heard of Him before.
I did not know how He looked.

I turned my head towards Him,
Standing where the flight of steps begins.
The priest said, "You may go in now."
I went up the stairs, unto Him.

It was just me and Him;
Just me, and Him,
Just, me and Him!
Just Him.

I stood staring
Until He made me sign
A pact with Him
For lifetimes to come.

On an *Ekadasi* morning
I met Him for the first time—
The One with a Conch,
Discus and Mace.

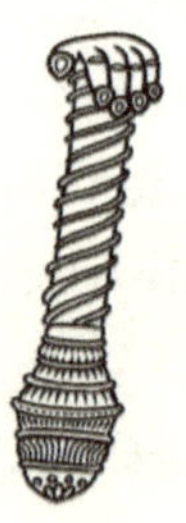

6.

They are both choosy actors,
They mind their entry points for the scene.
He emerged from Brahma's sacrificial fire,
She dwells in the *Bindu* of the *Sri Chakra*.

It's no ordinary sacrificial fire:
It's a culmination of blazing intent.
It's no ordinary central dot:
It's a coming together of one-pointed focus.

In fact, they will make their visits
To us too.
Only if we give them their entry points—
Intent; Focus.

They are already there, within us now.
For they have made our insides their abode;
For they have made our insides
the town of white *Gopurams*—Kanchipuram.

7.

She's an expert in double games;
And that's probably why
She has two pairs of hands.

She's an expert in double games.
Our mind and senses are in Her hands
As the sugarcane bow and flower arrows.
She leads us to fantasy worlds with those—
Mind and senses; bow and arrows.

She's an expert in double games.
The other pair keeps the noose and goad;
Just so that, when our expedition is done
And when it is time, She blocks our path
And pulls us to Her own abode.

She's an expert in double games—
The Sister of the Playful One at Kanchi.
With one pair of hands, She lays tests,
With the other pair, She rescues.

She's an expert in double games.

8.

You could hide
The lion of rage inside you;
You could hide even
The mammoth elephant of pride.

But you could never hide
Little butterflies of love
That flap their wings in the stomach,
Flutter all the way up to the bosom,
Tickle the neck, flush the cheeks,
And blossom in the eyes as a spark of smile.

Have you seen the face
Of our Mother who protects:
Perundevi—
The consort of Kanchi Varada,
Whose love for Her Lord
Would make even stones smile?

You could hide
The lion of rage inside you,
But never little butterflies
Of love.

9.

Siblings enjoy games together,
And this pair is no different.
They go one step further:
Their game board has been custom-made,
The coins have been carved with care,
Rules have been framed by them.
They are the Designers of the Game
And its Players too.

Siblings enjoy games together,
But these two play a Game
In which they are not opponents; but allies.
Allies who move coins together
On the game board called 'Universe'.
Siblings enjoy games together,
And this pair is no different.

10.

You gave me a heart to feel.
But when it melts in pain,
Who is to be blamed—You or me?
You gave me a mind to think.
But when it conjures illusory worlds,
Who is to be blamed—You or me?

You blessed me with words to speak.
But when it shoots irreversible daggers,
Who is to be blamed—You or me?
You blessed me with limbs to act.
But when it leaves behind baggage loads,
Who is to be blamed—You or me?

You are the Engineer,
O Empress of Shiva Kanchi,
The machine is yours;
When there is a malfunction,
The blame is on You. Not on me.

11.

He has something to do
With the waters.
The Milky Ocean is His abode.

He once dived down as a fish;
Then took the form of a tortoise;
Later bore the guise of a boar—
Lifted Bhoodevi from the depths of the sea.

He has something to do
With the waters.
The Milky Ocean is His abode.

Yamuna yearned to touch His toe—
That toe which Mother Ganges touches
Every day, every moment—
And that is probably why
She giggles, gurgles,
And moves about in gigantic strides.

He has something to do
With the waters.
The Milky Ocean is His abode.

He declared that He is verily Ganga—
That Ganga who dwells in the matted locks
Of the Lord of Shiva Kanchi.

He has something to do
With the waters—
The One, who devotees flock to worship
In Vishnu Kanchi.

12.

In the middle of the night,
When nobody is watching,
In the wink of an eye,
They exchange places—
He, who is tired of standing,
And His sister whose feet
Are numb of sitting cross-legged,
Exchange places.

Sometimes, they are still there
The next morning—you'll hardly realise.
They are proficient at it:
The act of exchanging places.
They did it once,
Between Mathura and Gokula;
But, this time, they do it
Well within the borders of
The temple town of white *Gopurams*—
Kanchipuram.

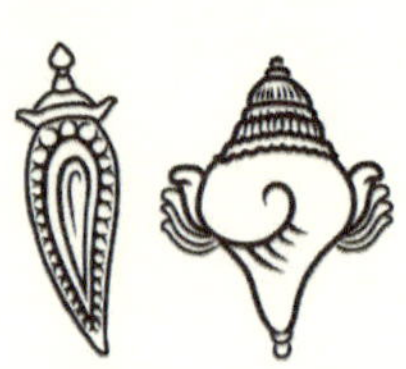

13.

It's hard to guess
Where Her glance is fixed:
The glance that fulfils desires.

Is Her glance slanted to the left,
Or, is She looking straight to the center?
Does She look from side to side,
In sync with the flame on the plate
In the priest's hand?

Seated in ease,
Right leg atop the left,
In the temple town of Kanchi;
It's hard to guess
Where Her glance is fixed—
The One whose eyes are everywhere.

When Her glance falls on us,
Desires are fulfilled.
When our glance falls on Her,
Desires are powdered.

14.

Beware!
Those without desires,
Those without thoughts,
Those seeking sheer joy—
Beware!
He's coming behind you,
Chasing you closely
At great speed.
Beware!

He has left behind
His conch, discus and mace;
He has left behind all comforts and
Pampering of devotees;
He has left behind the warmth
Of His blazing sanctum,
And is coming behind you
Amidst rain and storms.
Beware!

He has even left behind the great Devi—
Perundevi.
He has left the town of white *Gopurams*—
Kanchi,

To wash Himself
In the dust from thy feet.

Beware, those without desires!
Beware, those without thoughts!
He's coming behind you
Chasing you at great speed.

15.

It is best to beware
Of what we pray for
When in the town of white *Gopurams*.

Her name is Kamakshi;
Her glance fulfils desires.
His name is Varadaraja;
He is the all-giving King.
The place is Satyavrata Kshetra;
Where all vows attain completeness.

It is best to beware
Of what we pray for
When in the town of white *Gopurams*.

She is Kamakshi,
He is Varadaraja;
When we ask for one,
We will get back nine.

16.

People often ask, "Which came first—
The chicken or the egg?";
Now I ask, "Who came first—You or Me?
The deity or the devotee?"

If You gave birth to me,
Then You are responsible
For the course I take.
My scars are Your burden,
My smiles are Your little perks.

Who came first—You or Me?
The deity or the devotee?

If I gave birth to you,
Then, I have all the rights
To question you of your actions,
And, to scold;
For, you are Mine.

O Goddess, who silences questions
With a smile that is praised in verses a hundred,

Answer me now—
Who came first—You or Me?
The deity or the devotee?

44

17.

If you ever happen to be
In Varagiri*
On the third day of the festival
During Vaigasi,
Among the lakhs of pairs of eyes,
You will not miss to notice
One pair of eyes—
A pair of eyes that are wide;
Eyeballs in the middle
And whites all around.
Eyes that bear the image of the Lord;
Eyes that echo devotion;
Eyes that say "Make way!";
Eyes of the Veda; Eyes of Enlightenment.
But, what an irony are those pair of eyes,
When it cannot see for itself
The spectacle of the Lord's strides
On His majestic mount!

If you ever happen to be
In Varagiri
On the third day of the festival
During Vaigasi,
Among the lakhs of pairs of eyes,
You will not miss to notice

One pair of eyes—
That of His Eagle mount.

* Varagiri - Sanskrit name for Atthigiri

18.

There were three lines.

They seemed vertical at first,

Or were they actually horizontal?

If vertical and horizontal
Are only points of view,
Why then does the town have two halves—
Shiva Kanchi and Vishnu Kanchi?
When both are verily One,
But variegated by mere perspectives.

19.

Yesterday
i was asked to jump around
Like a monkey.
And i did.

Today
If i am asked to bray
Like a donkey,
i will do it. No other go.

Tomorrow
If i am asked to rule over a kingdom,
And the day after—
If i am asked to retire to a hermitage;

i may have to do it.
No other go. No other go.

If that is what
Has been designed
For me
By the Queen
Who dwells in Kanchi,

That alone is best for me.
i have to do it. No other go.

20.

Your devotees are spoilt
By You, verily.
There are no two ways about it.

You make them come to You
From miles away
Every other day
Leaving behind work and rest.

You smile at them;
A little differently than the last time;
Trap them and root them there,
Not letting them move.

You come to them,
As if You are one among them,
Eavesdrop, spy, and perform
Magic tricks like a Magician.

You are the One
Who has walked down
All the way from Vaikunta
With Your consort, serpent bed
And other allies. How smart of You!

Why can't You walk down further
And make our bodies Your Kanchipuram;
Make our hearts pure as Your white *Gopuram*;
Make the elephant mountain of ego submit to You,
And reside within us?

Your devotees are spoilt
By You, verily.
There are no two ways about it.

You make them come to You
From miles away
Every other day
Leaving behind work and rest.

21.

The town is in two:
Shiva Kanchi and Vishnu Kanchi.
But Her Brother also shares space
In Her residence.
The town is in two.

He has a small room
Close to Her,
And a private cottage
Well within Her quarters.
The town is in two.

In that private cottage,
There is a storey for Him to sit,
A space for Him to stand,
And a room where He reclines.
The town is in two.

If Shiva is verily She,
And She is verily Vishnu,
Connect the dots if you please.
The town is in two.

22.

Sometimes she hides behind
An array of flowers,
Sometimes, behind layers of sarees.
Sometimes, she is hidden beneath
A row of garlands affectionately adorned,
Or sometimes, under the nest of necklaces.
Sometimes, she hides below an armour
Of sandalwood paste,
Or sometimes even disguised with a
Piece of cloth stained with turmeric.
But, how long will she hide?—
The Mother who sits in an un-secluded sanctum
In Satyavrata Kshetram—Kanchipuram.
How long will she hide, when
Her smile and glance give her away at once?
How long will she hide, when
The child can easily sense the Mother's presence?

23.

O friend,
Will a thousand elephants suffice
To carry the blessings that he bestows?
Even an elephant's memory would fail
To remember his innumerable magical moves.

O friend,
He once rescued the elephant
That was caught in the clutches of a crocodile.
He is going to rescue us too
From the intoxicated elephants of this illusory world.

O friend,
He is the Mahout of our herd;
Go, fetch him like a King seated on an elephant.
He is Kari Varada—The one who is
The mighty Elephant atop
A humble elephant hill.

O friend with an elephant's gait,
Call out to him thus:
"Hurry! O Hari—needy's protector!"

24.

It's a now or never with Them.
If you want to make a move,
Do it right now; else,
End up staying rooted there
Forever.

They have a knack of
Looking into your eyes,
Boring into your being.

If you want to leave,
Do it now.
Show your back to Them
And walk ahead.

Their eyes follow you
Until you vanish from sight,
And even after.

So, if you have other work to do,
Take a sharp turn
And make a move.

For, it's a now or never
With the Siblings;
They look into your eyes
And bore into your being.

It's a now or never with Them.
If you want to make a move,
Do it right now.

25.

Don't be specific with demands.
Don't try to be smart.
The One who dwells in
The town of white *Gopurams*
Is smarter than us.

If we ask specific,
We will get back specific.
We might not be prepared.
The One who dwells in Kanchi
Is smarter than us.

What's given to us
Has been carefully handpicked.
Let's play a safe game; ask no more.
The One who dwells in Kanchi
Is smarter than us.

Don't be specific with demands.
Don't try to be smart.
The One who dwells in
The town of white *Gopurams*
Is smarter than us.

26.

He pulled me to the central core
Of the sacrificial fire.
He constructed a stage
In a space
That was already ablaze
With decades of chants of devotees.
In that heat of the fire,
He made me Dance to His Tunes.
The body was made to melt,
Ever-rising Ego was in ashes,
And I moved haphazardly like flames.
He pulled me to the central core
Of the sacrificial fire;
Made my body weak,
Mind: numb,
And made surrender the only option.
He placed me in His very abode,
Where He emerged out
Of Brahma's sacrificial fire.
He taught me what penance is,
And rung the bell when the class was done.

27.

The world of dreams
Is a parallel universe.

Sometimes, it's a different 'me'
Taking risks that I usually wouldn't dare to.
Talking back when I would usually be silent;
Being silent when I would want to speak.
Meeting new faces that are mostly a-blur;
Making new friends; bidding goodbye to some.

Stitching words together in ways
That I didn't know of earlier,
Creating a new vocabulary
Of movements in Dance,
Living a second life altogether
In my dreams; as if,
It was an alternate script
To the story of my life.

The world of dreams
Is a parallel universe,
Where sometimes,
The cross-legged Goddess of Kanchi
Reclines on the serpent bed in Rangam;

The reclining Lord seats Himself
On the throne in Thiruvarur;
The seated Lord seems to stand
With four arms in Kanchi;
And the standing Lord
Comfortably sits cross-legged
With a sugarcane bow and flower arrows
In the town of white *Gopurams*.

28.

Have you heard of a Sun
That rises in the West;
Have you heard of an orange fruit
That tastes spicy;
Have you heard of a river
That has no ripples;
Have you heard of a couple
That never disagree?

Have you heard of a life
That remains unchanged;
Have you heard of sandalwood
That gives out a stench;
Have you heard of a child
That overthinks;
Have you heard of an attachment
That is devoid of pain?

Have you heard of an owl
That sleeps at night;
Have you heard of a clock
That reverses time;
Have you heard of a bird
That flies backwards;

Have you heard of an old lady
That, like a baby, crawls?

Have you heard of snow
That feels hot;
Have you heard of a saint
That had a peaceful start;
Have you heard of a tree
That talks and walks;
Have you heard of the Empress
Of Kanchi—Kamakshi,
Who turns deaf ears to devotees' asks?

29.

The pond is nearby;
The elephant has to visit it
For his daily dose of water.
In that pond,
There are lotuses;
There are crocodiles too.

The pond is nearby,
The elephant's intent is on
The water and lotuses.
But, in that pond,
There are lotuses;
There are crocodiles too.

The crocodile in the pond
Grabs the leg of the elephant.
The elephant resists; fights back.
But, he cannot avoid that pond where
There are lotuses;
There are crocodiles too.

The elephant goes there again
Another day; the elephant is tired
Of fighting, resisting, wailing in pain.
But still, he has to make his visit to the pond where

There are lotuses;
There are crocodiles too.

One day, the elephant decides
To let go; to surrender.
He screams out the Lord's name—
Stuck in the grab of the crocodile in the pond where
There are lotuses;
There are crocodiles too.

The cries of the one with fan-like ears
Has reached the ears of the Lord in Vaikunta
Who whizzes down in great speed.
The earth below shakes; the skies above roar,
As the crocodile is cut asunder—
Liberated: elephant, thus the crocodile;
With His discus that whirls its way to the pond where
There are lotuses;
There are crocodiles too.

The elephant visits the pond still,
Every other day.
There are crocodiles still,
But the elephant no longer wails in pain,
For he has been freed.

The Lord now waits at the edge of His seat,
For the wail of the next elephant

That is about to visit the pond where
There are lotuses;
There are crocodiles too.

30.

Is this all meant to be mere trade?
And every move, a transaction?
Are we meant to be customers;
Counting penny for penny,
And building rich castles
With overdue loans?
Have you sent us here
For commerce? Give us an answer:
Partners in Business—
Siblings of Kanchipuram.

31.

The door is kept ajar.
Who will arrive first—
The Eagle or the Lion?
The windows are left open.
Which will come first—
The Discus or the Noose?
The space in my heart is vacant.
What should be built first—
A pedestal to stand,
Or a throne to sit?
O Siblings, who rush to rescue devotees;
Isn't it time yet?
Let your race begin.

32.

There are wars happening
And people rejoicing at the sight of blood.
Homes, lives, love and hope lost
And people dying a new death every day.
There are crimes all over
Of every possible kind,
And hatred strewn in plenty
As if they were available for free.
One cursing the other,
The other cursing another,
And the thread goes on loop.
There is pollution everywhere,
Air; water; sound; mind.
There are even tiny roaches
In your sanctum-sanctorums;
Yet you stand & sit respectively—
O Brother & Sister,
And smile.

33.

Brahma spearheaded the *Yagna*
And Vishnu was the One who emerged out;
Shakti dwells there as Kamakshi
And Her husband sits alone under a tree;
The Goddess who plays the lute
Gushed there as River Vegavathi;
And the Goddess of wealth
Is everywhere where Her Lord is,
In that town where the deities who
Create
Protect
Destroy
Come together—
In Kanchipuri: the town of white *Gopurams.*
In that town where
Brahmaloka
Vaikunta
Kailasa
Come together—
In Kanchipuri: the town of white *Gopurams.*

● ● ●

A NOTE OF GRATITUDE

Gratitude, I believe, is one of the most intricate of emotions to experience. As I stand at the seemingly blur finish line of this marathon of marvel, I wonder if this is only a beginning of yet another beautiful journey, carefully curated by the Divine Siblings.

If it comes,
It comes.
If it doesn't,
It doesn't.
That's how it is: Poetry.

The muses have taught me to wait, to be patient and value the process of creativity—be it in Dance or Writing. They have given me gentle pats on the back and some benign smiles as rewards for my patience. I consider this book of poems to be one such precious reward from them.

I begin my expression of utmost gratitude by offering reverential prostrations to **Pujyasri Ramanacharana Tirtha Swami**, whose profound discourse on *Shivanandalahari* revealed to me the Mantra from the Rudrahṛdayopaniṣad—"yā umā sā svayaṃ visnuḥ"—thereby, providentially paving the path to this poetry anthology.

The Siblings of Kanchipuram—'they are tricksters'; they 'enjoy games together'; they are 'partners in business', indeed.

I am grateful to the Siblings for bestowing a timely gift—
Smaran Haridashwa, at the eleventh hour—who, through
his knowledge of the scriptures, love for poetry and a taste
for *Bhakti,* has given his all for this book, as if it were his own.
His pure intent, crystallised as profound ideas, manifests as a
befitting 'Invocation' to this anthology. This work of art that
stemmed from my heart has earned more beauty through
the finishing touches and meaningful edits that Smaran has
made. He reviewed this text with the lens of clarity and a sense
of magnanimity, admiring the 'garland' at exquisite detail and
restringing it, as need be. At this crucial juncture, I cannot
help but gape with wonder at the journey that this book has
traversed—from its inception, born of the Guru's Grace, to its
completion, at the very hands of his ardent disciple.

I express my heartfelt thanks to Latha ma'am (**Ms. Latha K.**)
who gave me the nudge of confidence to bring these poems
out as a collection and for being a strong pillar of support
all through the process. I present my salutations to **Sujatha
Vijayaraghavan ma'am** whose words of encouragement
to me in the Foreword have become an impetus to work
harder. I am immensely thankful to her and Natyarangam
for being a channel for Varadar's impactful entry into my life,
strengthening the bond between *Bhakti* and Art for me.

My thanks are due to two artists whose craft has lent colour
to the book. It is one thing to have ideas, and an entirely
different thing to put it into action. Avanti *akka* (**Mrs. Avanti
Natarajan**), The Art Brew-Creative Company, has intricately
designed this book's cover, and designed the interiors of

the book with her eye for nuances, quite literally binding it with a heart full of passion. The suggestive representation of the Siblings through simple symbols have been sketched sincerely by **Meghna Unnikrishnan**.

I am indebted to my parents, teachers, family and friends who always stand by me through highs and lows. To dear Sudhavalli, Sharanya, Rajeevi and the little ones who make me feel at home at Kanchi; to the driver *annas* who drive me back and forth to Kanchi, even at odd times of the day—I place my thanks. To Notion Press, for their support in publishing my second anthology—I pay my thanks.

The expanse of skies fills my eyes,
The chirping of birds fills my ears,
Swelling gratitude fills my heart;
And the time is just ripe
To think of the gods
That have given me the Gift of Dance;
To think of the planets
That have shown me the World of Literature;
To think of the stars
That have sown in me a Passion for Poetry;
And to think of the roads
That lead me to the town of white *Gopurams*—
Kanchipuram.

Harinie Jeevitha
22-08-24

With prayerful prostrations at the lotus feet of Mahaperiyava—the Paramacharya of Kanchipuram.